TRADITIONAL FAMILY CAKES

TRADITIONAL FAMILY CAKES

First edition published in 2011

LOVE FOOD is an imprint of Parragon Books Ltd

Parragon
Queen Street House
4 Queen Street
Bath BA1 1HE, UK

www.parragon.com

ISBN: 978-1-4454-2295-4

Printed in China

Cover and new photography by Clive Streeter
Home economy and new recipes by Angela Drake

Notes for the Reader
This book uses both metric and imperial measurements. Follow the same units of measurement throughout; do not mix metric and imperial. All spoon measurements are level: teaspoons are assumed to be 5 ml, and tablespoons are assumed to be 15 ml. Unless otherwise stated, milk is assumed to be full fat, eggs and individual vegetables are medium, and pepper is freshly ground black pepper.

The times given are an approximate guide only. Preparation times differ according to the techniques used by different people and the cooking times may also vary from those given. Optional ingredients, variations or serving suggestions have not been included in the calculations.

Recipes using raw or very lightly cooked eggs should be avoided by infants, the elderly, pregnant women, convalescents and anyone suffering from an illness. Pregnant and breastfeeding women are advised to avoid eating peanuts and peanut products. Sufferers from nut allergies should be aware that some of the ready-made ingredients used in the recipes in this book may contain nuts. Always check the packaging before use.

Contents

Introduction

From a simple jam-filled Victoria Sponge Cake to a moist and sticky iced Gingerbread, luscious Lemon Drizzle Cake or an indulgent Chocolate Gateau, nothing can beat the flavour of a home-made cake. The wonderful aroma that fills the air from a warm kitchen and the satisfaction of presenting your own creation to family or friends is so rewarding that it's no wonder that home baking is as popular now as it ever was.

This book contains a collection of traditional cake recipes that are easy to make with clear instructions and simple icings and decorations. Whether it's a mid-morning coffee, afternoon tea, birthday treat or a special celebration, you'll find a cake to fit the occasion.

The Basic Ingredients

As with any type of cooking it's worth buying good quality basic ingredients. For the best flavour, choose a lightly salted or unsalted butter. Soft margarine can be used instead of butter, but avoid low-fat spreads as they have a high water content and an inferior taste.

Always use the correct-sized egg. Unless specified, all the recipes in this book use medium eggs. Allow the eggs to come to room temperature for about 1 hour before using.

Check that flours and raising agents are not past their sell-by date. Stale flour will impart an unpleasant taste and raising agents can lose their effectiveness resulting in a heavy textured cake.

Caster sugar is the most popular sugar for cake making – its fine grains dissolve easily when creamed with butter. To make your own vanilla sugar, simply pop a vanilla pod in a container of caster sugar and leave for 5–6 days. Chocolate and darker fruit cakes are often made with soft brown sugars or unrefined muscovado sugar as they give a richer colour and flavour.

Essential Equipment

Any reasonably equipped kitchen should have most of the basics needed for cake making – bowls, spoons, spatulas, a sieve and a wire rack for cooling. A good set of measuring scales to ensure accurate weighing is also essential and a handheld electric mixer will make light work of creaming and whisking.

The only other major items to buy are the appropriate-sized cake tins. You'll need a range of shapes and sizes so you'll probably have to build up your collection gradually. When buying, pick sturdy cake tins that will last – flimsy tins may buckle quickly and have to be replaced. If you buy tins with a non-stick coating, take care not to scratch the lining with metal utensils. Always wash tins thoroughly after use and place in a warm oven to dry out completely before putting away. An alternative to metal tins is to try flexible non-stick silicone bakeware – you'll find a good range of shapes, sizes and colours and they are easy to use and clean.

Secrets of Success

Always read the recipe before you start baking. Make sure that you have all the ingredients to hand (at room temperature, if necessary). Weigh out the ingredients accurately – this is especially important with raising agents, such as baking powder or bicarbonate of soda, as too much or too little can have a drastic effect on the finished cake.

Before turning on the oven, make sure the shelves are in the correct position. Allow at least 10 minutes for the oven to preheat to the required temperature. If you have a fan oven, check the manufacturers' instructions – you may need to reduce the temperature by 10–20°C/50–68°F. Once the cake is in the oven, don't be tempted to open the door too soon or too often as the cold air will lower the temperature and the cake may sink.

Take time to prepare the correct-sized cake tin. Lightly grease with melted butter or a flavourless cooking oil then line with baking paper, cutting to fit neatly.

There are two ways to test whether a cake is cooked. For a light sponge cake, simply press the top of the cake gently with your fingertips. The cake should feel springy to the touch and give very lightly, leaving no imprint. For richer cakes or fruit cakes, it's best to insert a thin skewer into the centre of the cake, then pull it out quickly – the skewer should come away clean. If there is any cake mixture sticking to the skewer then return the cake to the oven and bake for a little longer.

Freshly baked cakes are very fragile so leave them to cool in the tin for 5–15 minutes before turning them out. Run a thin-bladed palette knife around the edge of the tin to loosen the cake before inverting onto a wire rack. To prevent marks on the top of delicate sponges, quickly flip them onto another rack. Let rich fruit cakes cool completely in the tin before turning out.

Common Cake Dilemmas

- If the cake has sunk in the middle – has too much raising agent been used, the oven door been opened too soon or the cake not been cooked for long enough?
- If the cake has a dry and crumbly texture – has the cake been cooked for too long or has too much baking powder been used?
- If the dried fruit sinks to the bottom of cake – is the cake mixture too slack or the oven temperature too low?
- If the cake has not risen – has too little raising agent been used or has the cake mixture been over-whisked/beaten?
- Always make sure the cake is completely cold before storing it in an airtight tin. If the cake is still a little warm condensation may form which can cause mould to grow on the surface.
- If the cake has a fresh cream or soft cheese filling or icing, it will need to be stored in the refrigerator but allow it to stand at room temperature for about 30 minutes before serving.
- Some cakes, such as gingerbread, will improve in flavour if kept for a few days before serving. Wrap well in greaseproof paper and then foil to prevent them from drying out.
- Many cakes freeze well. Place in large freezer bags or wrap in foil, excluding as much air as possible. Unwrap before defrosting and leave at room temperature to defrost thoroughly.

CLASSIC CAKES

1

Chocolate Fudge Cake

SERVES 8

◆ Cooking time:
30–35 minutes

INGREDIENTS

✷ 175 g/6 oz unsalted
butter, softened, plus
extra for greasing
✷ 175 g/6 oz golden
caster sugar
✷ 3 eggs, beaten
✷ 3 tbsp golden syrup
✷ 40 g/1½ oz ground
almonds
✷ 175 g/6 oz self-raising
flour
✷ pinch of salt
✷ 40 g/1½ oz cocoa
powder

ICING

✷ 225 g/8 oz plain
chocolate, broken
into pieces
✷ 55 g/2 oz dark
muscovado sugar
✷ 225 g/8 oz unsalted
butter, diced
✷ 5 tbsp evaporated milk
✷ ½ tsp vanilla extract

Everyone loves a good chocolate cake and this moist chocolate cake smothered in a rich fudge frosting is one of the best! It is ideal for serving at a special celebration or as a delicious chocolate dessert.

1. Preheat the oven to 180°C/350°F/Gas Mark 4. Grease and line two 20-cm/8-inch sandwich tins.

2. To make the icing, place the chocolate, muscovado sugar, butter, evaporated milk and vanilla extract in a heavy-based saucepan. Heat gently, stirring constantly, until melted. Pour into a bowl and leave to cool. Cover and chill in the refrigerator for 1 hour, or until spreadable.

3. For the cake, place the butter and caster sugar in a bowl and beat together until light and fluffy. Gradually beat in the eggs. Stir in the golden syrup and ground almonds. Sift the flour, salt and cocoa powder into a separate bowl, then fold into the mixture. Add a little water, if necessary, to make a dropping consistency.

4. Spoon the mixture into the prepared tins and bake in the preheated oven for 30–35 minutes, or until springy to the touch and a skewer inserted in the centre comes out clean.

5. Leave the cakes in the tins for 5 minutes, then turn out onto wire racks to cool completely. When the cakes are cold, sandwich them together with half the icing. Spread the remaining icing over the top and sides of the cake, swirling it to give a frosted appearance.

TOP TIP
Use a small palette knife to swirl
the frosting evenly over the top and
sides of the cake.

Lemon Drizzle Cake

SERVES 8

✦ Cooking time:
45–60 minutes

INGREDIENTS

✳ butter, for greasing
✳ 200 g/7 oz plain flour
✳ 2 tsp baking powder
✳ 200 g/7 oz caster sugar
✳ 4 eggs
✳ 150 ml/5 fl oz soured cream
✳ grated rind of 1 large lemon
✳ 4 tbsp lemon juice
✳ 150 ml/5 fl oz sunflower oil

SYRUP

✳ 4 tbsp icing sugar
✳ 3 tbsp lemon juice

This cake has a tangy lemon sugar syrup drizzled over it while still warm which permeates through the sponge to give it a wonderful moistness and extra lemony flavour.

1. Preheat the oven to 180°C/350°F/Gas Mark 4. Grease and line a 20-cm/8-inch loose-bottomed round cake tin.

2. Sift the flour and baking powder into a mixing bowl and stir in the caster sugar.

3. In a separate bowl, whisk the eggs, soured cream, lemon rind, lemon juice and oil together.

4. Pour the egg mixture into the dry ingredients and mix well until evenly combined.

5. Pour the mixture into the prepared tin and bake in the preheated oven for 45–60 minutes, or until risen and golden brown.

6. Meanwhile, to make the syrup, mix together the icing sugar and lemon juice in a small saucepan. Stir over a low heat until just beginning to bubble and turn syrupy.

7. As soon as the cake comes out of the oven, prick the surface with a fine skewer, then brush the syrup over the top. Leave the cake to cool completely in the tin before turning out and serving.

TOP TIP

For a crunchy lemon crust, make the lemon syrup with granulated sugar instead of icing sugar.

Carrot Cake

SERVES 10

◆ Cooking time:
1 hour–1 hour 10 minutes

INGREDIENTS

✳ oil or melted butter,
for greasing

✳ 175 g/6 oz plain
white flour

✳ 1 tbsp baking powder

✳ 1 tsp ground cinnamon

✳ ½ tsp ground ginger

✳ 175 g/6 oz unsalted
butter, softened

✳ 175 g/6 oz light
muscovado sugar

✳ 3 eggs, beaten

✳ 2 tbsp orange juice

✳ 200 g/7 oz carrots,
roughly grated

✳ 55 g/2 oz pecan nuts,
chopped, plus extra pecan
halves to decorate

FROSTING

✳ 55 g/2 oz full-fat
soft cheese

✳ 250 g/9 oz icing sugar

✳ finely grated rind of
1 orange

✳ 1 tbsp orange juice,
plus extra if needed

Sometimes called Passion Cake, this classic teatime treat is made with grated carrots which soften during baking to give a deliciously moist texture and sweet flavour. Once iced, this cake is best kept in the refrigerator but allow it to stand at room temperature for at least 30 minutes before serving.

1. Preheat the oven to 160°C/325°F/Gas Mark 3. Grease and line a 23-cm/9-inch round deep cake tin.

2. Sift the flour, baking powder, cinnamon and ginger into a bowl and add the butter, muscovado sugar and eggs. Beat well until smooth, then stir in the orange juice, carrots and chopped pecan nuts.

3. Spoon the mixture into the prepared tin and smooth the surface. Bake in the preheated oven for 1 hour–1 hour 10 minutes, or until risen, firm and golden brown.

4. Leave to cool in the tin for 10 minutes, then turn out onto a wire rack to finish cooling. For the frosting, place all the ingredients in a bowl and beat until smooth and thick, adding more orange juice if necessary. Spread over the top of the cake and decorate with pecan halves.

TOP TIP

Instead of the pecan nuts, decorate with tiny carrots shaped from orange-coloured marzipan or sugar paste.

Coffee & Walnut Cake

SERVES 8

◆ Cooking time:
20–25 minutes

INGREDIENTS

✳ 175 g/6 oz unsalted
butter, plus extra
for greasing
✳ 175 g/6 oz light
muscovado sugar
✳ 3 large eggs, beaten
✳ 3 tbsp strong
black coffee
✳ 175 g/6 oz self-raising
flour
✳ 1½ tsp baking powder
✳ 115 g/4 oz walnut
pieces
✳ walnut halves,
to decorate

FROSTING

✳ 115 g/4 oz unsalted
butter
✳ 200 g/7 oz icing sugar
✳ 1 tbsp strong
black coffee
✳ ½ tsp vanilla extract

Coffee and walnuts complement each other perfectly in this much loved sandwich cake. The sponges are packed with chopped walnuts and the creamy coffee frosting has just the right touch of sweetness.

1. Preheat the oven to 180°C/350°F/Gas Mark 4. Grease and line two 20-cm/8-inch sandwich tins.

2. Beat the butter and muscovado sugar together until pale and fluffy. Gradually add the eggs, beating well after each addition. Beat in the coffee.

3. Sift the flour and baking powder into the mixture, then fold in lightly and evenly with a metal spoon. Fold in the walnut pieces. Divide the mixture between the prepared cake tins and smooth the surfaces. Bake in the preheated oven for 20–25 minutes, or until golden brown and springy to the touch. Turn out onto a wire rack to cool.

4. For the frosting, beat together the butter, icing sugar, coffee and vanilla extract, mixing until smooth and creamy.

5. Use about half the mixture to sandwich the cakes together, then spread the remaining frosting on top and swirl with a palette knife. Decorate with walnut halves.

TOP TIP
For the best flavour use a
strong espresso coffee or a good
quality strong instant coffee powder.

Iced Madeira Cake

SERVES 8–10

◆ Cooking time:
1–1¼ hours

INGREDIENTS

✳ 175 g/6 oz unsalted
butter, softened, plus
extra for greasing

✳ 175 g/6 oz caster sugar

✳ finely grated rind of
1 lemon

✳ 3 eggs, lightly beaten

✳ 140 g/5 oz self-raising
flour

✳ 115 g/4 oz plain flour

✳ 2 tbsp milk

✳ 1 tbsp lemon juice

ICING

✳ 175 g/6 oz icing sugar

✳ 2–3 tbsp lemon juice

✳ 2 tsp lemon curd,
warmed

Named after the wine it was traditionally served with, this classic sponge cake has a fairly firm texture with a buttery flavour. Topped with a tangy lemon icing, it makes the perfect teatime treat.

1. Preheat the oven to 160°C/325°F/Gas Mark 3. Grease and line a 900-g/2-lb loaf tin.

2. Place the butter and caster sugar in a large bowl and beat together until very pale and fluffy. Beat in the lemon rind then gradually beat in the eggs.

3. Sift the self-raising and plain flour into the mixture and fold in gently until thoroughly incorporated. Fold in the milk and lemon juice.

4. Spoon the mixture into the prepared tin and bake in the preheated oven for 1–1¼ hours, or until well risen, golden brown and a skewer inserted into the centre comes out clean. Cool in the tin for 15 minutes, then turn out onto a wire rack to cool completely.

5. For the icing, sift the icing sugar into a bowl. Add the lemon juice and stir to make a smooth and thick icing. Gently spread the icing over the top of the cake. Drizzle the warmed lemon curd over the icing and drag a skewer through the icing to create a swirled effect. Leave to set.

TOP TIP
Cover the top of the
cake loosely with foil after about
50 minutes to prevent over-browning.

Classic Cherry Cake

SERVES 8

♦ Cooking time:
1–1¼ hours

INGREDIENTS

✳ 250 g/9 oz glacé
cherries, quartered

✳ 85 g/3 oz ground
almonds

✳ 200 g/7 oz plain flour

✳ 1 tsp baking powder

✳ 200 g/7 oz unsalted
butter, plus extra
for greasing

✳ 200 g/7 oz caster sugar

✳ 3 large eggs

✳ finely grated rind and
juice of 1 lemon

✳ 6 sugar cubes, crushed

This traditional favourite is dotted with sweet red glacé cherries, flavoured with lemon rind and juice and topped with crushed sugar cubes. The trick to stopping the cherries from sinking to the bottom during baking is to wash and dry them thoroughly before using to remove the sticky glaze.

1. Preheat the oven to 180°C/350°F/Gas Mark 4. Grease and line a 20-cm/8-inch round cake tin.

2. Stir together the cherries, ground almonds and 1 tablespoon of the flour. Sift the remaining flour into a separate bowl with the baking powder.

3. Beat the butter and sugar together until light in colour and fluffy in texture. Gradually add the eggs, beating hard with each addition, until evenly mixed.

4. Add the flour mixture and fold lightly and evenly into the creamed mixture with a metal spoon. Add the cherry mixture and fold in evenly. Finally, fold in the lemon rind and juice.

5. Spoon the mixture into the prepared cake tin and sprinkle with the crushed sugar cubes. Bake in the preheated oven for 1–1¼ hours, or until risen, golden brown and the cake is just beginning to shrink away from the sides of the tin.

6. Cool in the tin for about 15 minutes, then turn out to finish cooling on a wire rack.

TOP TIP
If the mixture starts to curdle when beating in the eggs, add a spoonful of the flour.

Glazed Gingerbread

SERVES 12

◆ Cooking time:
1–1¼ hours

INGREDIENTS

✳ 250 g/9 oz plain flour
✳ 1 tsp bicarbonate of soda
✳ 1½ tsp ground ginger
✳ 1 tsp ground mixed spice
✳ 115 g/4 oz butter, plus extra for greasing
✳ 115 g/4 oz light muscovado sugar
✳ 150 g/5½ oz golden syrup
✳ 85 g/3 oz black treacle
✳ 2 large eggs, beaten
✳ 2 tbsp milk

ICING

✳ 115 g/4 oz icing sugar
✳ 1 tbsp stem ginger syrup
✳ 1–2 tbsp water
✳ 1 piece stem ginger, finely chopped

The flavour of this cake will improve with time. If you have the patience, wrap the un-iced cake in greaseproof paper and store in a cool place for a few days before icing.

1. Preheat the oven to 160°C/325°F/Gas Mark 3. Grease and line an 18-cm/7-inch square cake tin.

2. Sift the flour, bicarbonate of soda, ground ginger and mixed spice into a large bowl. Place the butter, sugar, golden syrup and black treacle in pan and heat gently, stirring all the time, until the butter has melted. Cool for 5 minutes.

3. Stir the melted mixture into the bowl and mix well. Add the eggs and milk and beat until thoroughly incorporated.

4. Spoon the mixture into the prepared tin and bake in the preheated oven for 1–1¼ hours, or until well risen and firm to the touch. Cool in the tin for 15 minutes then turn out onto a wire rack to cool completely.

5. For the icing, sift the icing sugar into a bowl. Stir in the stem ginger syrup and enough of the water to make a smooth icing that just coats the back of a wooden spoon.

6. Spoon the icing over the top of the cake, allowing it to run down the sides. Scatter over the stem ginger and leave to set.

TOP TIP

For a fruity flavour, top the gingerbread mixture with thin slices of apple before baking.

2

4

6

Victoria Sponge Cake

SERVES 8

◆ Cooking time:
25–30 minutes

INGREDIENTS

✺ 175 g/6 oz self-raising
flour
✺ 1 tsp baking powder
✺ 175 g/6 oz butter,
softened, plus extra
for greasing
✺ 175 g/6 oz golden
caster sugar
✺ 3 eggs
✺ icing sugar, for dusting

FILLING

✺ 3 tbsp raspberry jam
✺ 300 ml/10 fl oz double
cream, whipped
✺ 16 fresh strawberries,
halved

Named after Queen Victoria, this classic sandwich cake is given the star treatment with a luxurious filling of jam, softly whipped cream and fresh strawberries. Just perfect for a summer afternoon tea.

1. Preheat the oven to 180°C/350°F/Gas Mark 4. Grease and line two 20-cm/8-inch sandwich tins.

2. Sift the flour and baking powder into a bowl and add the butter, sugar and eggs. Mix together, then beat well until smooth.

3. Divide the mixture evenly between the prepared tins and smooth the surfaces. Bake in the preheated oven for 25–30 minutes, or until well risen and golden brown, and the cakes feel springy when lightly pressed.

4. Leave to cool in the tins for 5 minutes, then turn out and peel off the lining paper. Transfer to wire racks to cool completely. Sandwich the cakes together with the raspberry jam, whipped double cream and strawberry halves. Dust with icing sugar and serve.

TOP TIP
To create a lacy pattern on the top of the cake, place a paper doily over the top of the cake, dust with icing sugar then carefully lift the paper away.

Date & Walnut Loaf

SERVES 8

✦ Cooking time:
35–40 minutes

INGREDIENTS

✳ 100 g/3½ oz dates,
stoned and chopped

✳ ½ tsp bicarbonate
of soda

✳ finely grated rind of
½ lemon

✳ 100 ml/3½ fl oz hot tea

✳ 40 g/1½ oz unsalted
butter, plus extra
for greasing

✳ 70 g/2½ oz light
muscovado sugar

✳ 1 small egg

✳ 125 g/4½ oz self-
raising flour

✳ 25 g/1 oz walnuts,
chopped

✳ walnut halves,
to decorate

Dried dates soaked in hot tea until softened give this loaf a lovely moist and crumbly texture. It is delicious when lightly spread with unsalted butter.

1. Preheat the oven to 180°C/350°F/Gas Mark 4. Grease and line a 450-g/1-lb loaf tin.

2. Place the dates, bicarbonate of soda and lemon rind in a bowl and add the hot tea. Leave to soak for 10 minutes until softened.

3. Beat the butter and sugar together until light and fluffy, then beat in the egg. Stir the date mixture into this butter mixture.

4. Fold in the flour using a large metal spoon, then fold in the walnuts. Spoon the mixture into the prepared cake tin and smooth the surface. Top with the walnut halves.

5. Bake in the preheated oven for 35–40 minutes, or until risen, firm and golden brown. Cool for 10 minutes in the tin, then turn out onto a wire rack to cool completely.

TOP TIP

Choose a fragrant tea for soaking the dates, such as Earl Grey, or use a good quality English Breakfast Tea.

FRUIT & NUT CAKES

2

Rich Fruit Cake

SERVES 16

◆ Cooking time:
2¼–2¾ hours

INGREDIENTS

✳ 350 g/12 oz sultanas

✳ 225 g/8 oz raisins

✳ 115 g/4 oz ready-to-eat dried apricots, chopped

✳ 85 g/3 oz stoned dates, chopped

✳ 4 tbsp dark rum or brandy, plus extra for flavouring (optional)

✳ finely grated rind and juice of 1 orange

✳ 225 g/8 oz unsalted butter, plus extra for greasing

✳ 225 g/8 oz light muscovado sugar

✳ 4 eggs

✳ 70 g/2½ oz chopped mixed peel

✳ 85 g/3 oz glacé cherries, quartered

✳ 25 g/1 oz chopped glacé ginger or stem ginger

✳ 40 g/1½ oz blanched almonds, chopped

✳ 200 g/7 oz plain flour

✳ 1 tsp ground mixed spice

The cake of choice for celebrations, such as weddings and Christmas, this classic favourite should be made well in advance to allow time for the rich flavours to mature.

1. Place the sultanas, raisins, apricots and dates in a large bowl and stir in the rum, orange rind and orange juice. Cover and leave to soak for several hours or overnight.

2. Preheat the oven to 150°C/300°F/Gas Mark 2. Grease and line a 20-cm/8-inch round deep cake tin.

3. Beat the butter and sugar together until light and fluffy. Gradually beat in the eggs, beating hard after each addition. Stir in the soaked fruits, mixed peel, glacé cherries, glacé ginger and blanched almonds.

4. Sift the flour and mixed spice, then fold lightly and evenly into the mixture. Spoon the mixture into the prepared cake tin and smooth the surface, making a slight depression in the centre with the back of the spoon.

5. Bake in the preheated oven for 2¼–2¾ hours, or until the cake is beginning to shrink away from the sides and a skewer inserted into the centre comes out clean. Cool completely in the tin.

6. Turn out the cake and remove the lining paper. Wrap in greaseproof paper and foil, and store for at least two months before use. To add a richer flavour, prick the cake with a skewer and spoon over a couple of extra tablespoons of rum or brandy, if using, before storing.

TOP TIP
Make sure to wrap the cake
well before storing. Keep in a dry,
cool place.

Orange & Poppy Seed Cake

SERVES 10

◆ Cooking time:
45–50 minutes

INGREDIENTS

✳ 200 g/7 oz unsalted butter, plus extra for greasing

✳ 200 g/7 oz golden caster sugar

✳ 3 large eggs, beaten

✳ finely grated rind of 1 orange

✳ 55 g/2 oz poppy seeds

✳ 300 g/10½ oz plain flour, plus extra for dusting

✳ 2 tsp baking powder

✳ 150 ml/5 fl oz milk

✳ 125 ml/4 fl oz orange juice

✳ strips of orange zest, to decorate

SYRUP

✳ 140 g/5 oz golden caster sugar

✳ 150 ml/5 fl oz orange juice

Popular in North America, bundt cakes are named after the distinctive ring-shaped tins they are baked in. This version has a lovely soft sponge full of poppy seeds and soaked in a sweet orange syrup.

1. Preheat the oven to 160°C/325°F/Gas Mark 3. Grease and lightly flour a Bundt ring tin, about 24 cm/9 inches in diameter and with a capacity of approximately 2 litres/3½ pints.

2. Beat the butter and sugar together until pale and fluffy, then add the eggs gradually, beating thoroughly after each addition. Stir in the orange rind and poppy seeds. Sift in the flour and baking powder, then fold in evenly. Add the milk and orange juice, stirring to mix evenly.

3. Spoon the mixture into the prepared tin and bake in the preheated oven for 45–50 minutes, or until firm and golden brown. Leave to cool in the tin for 10 minutes, then turn out onto a wire rack to cool.

4. For the syrup, place the sugar and orange juice in a saucepan and heat gently until the sugar melts. Bring to the boil and simmer for about 5 minutes, or until reduced and syrupy. Spoon the syrup over the cake while it is still warm. Top with the strips of orange zest and serve warm or cold.

TOP TIP

Take extra care when turning the cake out onto the wire rack. If the sponge sticks a little, then gently ease it away from the tin with tip of a spatula.

Clementine Cake

SERVES 8

◆ Cooking time:
55–60 minutes

INGREDIENTS

✻ 2 clementines
✻ 175 g/6 oz butter, softened, plus extra for greasing
✻ 175 g/6 oz caster sugar
✻ 3 eggs, beaten
✻ 175 g/6 oz self-raising flour
✻ 3 tbsp ground almonds
✻ 3 tbsp single cream

GLAZE & TOPPING

✻ 6 tbsp clementine juice
✻ 2 tbsp caster sugar
✻ 3 white sugar cubes, crushed

Topped with a sweet orange glaze and crushed sugar cubes, this impressive cake makes a great dessert served warm with a spoonful of Greek yogurt or crème fraîche.

1. Preheat the oven to 180°C/350°F/Gas Mark 4. Grease and line an 18-cm/7-inch round cake tin.

2. Pare the rind from the clementines and chop the rind finely. In a bowl, cream together the butter, sugar and clementine rind until pale and fluffy.

3. Gradually add the beaten eggs to the mixture, beating thoroughly after each addition.

4. Gently fold in the self-raising flour followed by the ground almonds and the single cream. Spoon the mixture into the prepared tin.

5. Bake in the preheated oven for 55–60 minutes, or until a fine skewer inserted into the centre comes out clean. Leave in the tin to cool slightly.

6. Meanwhile, make the glaze. Put the clementine juice into a small saucepan with the caster sugar. Bring to the boil and simmer for 5 minutes.

7. Transfer the cake to a wire rack. Drizzle the glaze over the cake until it has been absorbed and sprinkle with the crushed sugar cubes.

TOP TIP

If clementines are unavailable, use small oranges or satsumas instead.

Spiced Apple Cake

SERVES 8–10

◆ Cooking time:
1–1¼ hours

INGREDIENTS

✳ 225 g/8 oz unsalted butter, softened, plus extra for greasing

✳ 225 g/8 oz light muscovado sugar

✳ 4 large eggs, lightly beaten

✳ 225 g/8 oz self-raising flour

✳ 2 tsp ground cinnamon

✳ ½ tsp grated nutmeg

✳ 85 g/3 oz sultanas

✳ 3 small dessert apples, peeled, cored and thinly sliced

✳ 2 tbsp clear honey, warmed

A lightly spiced sponge full of sultanas and apples with a sweet honey glaze, this cake will stay moist and delicious for up to a week.

1. Preheat the oven to 180°C/350°F/Gas Mark 4. Grease and line a 23-cm/9-inch round springform cake tin.

2. Place the butter and sugar in a large bowl and beat together until light and fluffy. Gradually beat in the eggs. Sift the flour, cinnamon and nutmeg into the mixture and fold in gently using a metal spoon. Fold in the sultanas.

3. Spoon half the mixture into the prepared tin and smooth the surface. Scatter over half the sliced apples. Spoon over the rest of the cake mixture and gently smooth the surface. Arrange the rest of the apple slices over the top.

4. Bake in the preheated oven for 1–1¼ hours, or until risen, golden brown and firm to the touch. Leave to cool in the tin for 10 minutes then turn out to cool on a wire rack. Brush the top with the warmed honey and leave to cool completely.

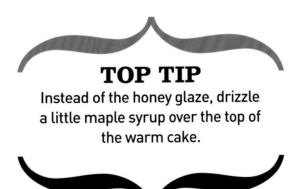

TOP TIP
Instead of the honey glaze, drizzle a little maple syrup over the top of the warm cake.

Fruit & Nut Loaf

SERVES 8–10

◆ Cooking time:
1–1¼ hours

INGREDIENTS

✺ 175 g/6 oz butter, softened, plus extra for greasing

✺ 115 g/4 oz light muscovado sugar

✺ 2 tbsp set honey

✺ 3 eggs, beaten

✺ 200 g/7 oz wholemeal self-raising flour

✺ ½ tsp baking powder

✺ 115 g/4 oz sultanas

✺ 85 g/3 oz ready-to-eat dried apricots, chopped

✺ 85 g/3 oz glacé cherries, quartered

✺ 25 g/1 oz walnuts, roughly chopped

✺ 25 g/1 oz macadamia nuts, roughly chopped

BUTTERCREAM

✺ 85 g/3 oz unsalted butter, softened

✺ 2 tsp finely grated orange rind

✺ 1 tbsp orange juice

✺ 175 g/6 oz icing sugar

Wholemeal flour, honey, dried fruits and nuts combine to make this wonderful wholesome fruit cake – just right for a mid-morning pick-me-up!

1. Preheat the oven to 160°C/325°F/Gas Mark 3. Grease and line a 900-g/2-lb loaf tin.

2. Place the butter, sugar and honey in a large bowl and beat together until very pale and fluffy. Gradually beat in the eggs.

3. Sift the flour and baking powder into the mixture, tipping any bran left in the sieve into the bowl. Fold in gently until thoroughly incorporated. Fold in the fruit and nuts.

4. Spoon the mixture into the prepared tin and gently smooth the surface. Bake in the preheated oven for 45 minutes then cover the top loosely with foil. Bake for a further 20–30 minutes, or until golden brown and a skewer inserted into the centre comes out clean. Cool in the tin for 15 minutes, then turn out onto a wire rack to cool completely.

5. For the buttercream, place the butter, orange rind and juice in a bowl and beat together until smooth. Gradually beat in the icing sugar. Spread over the top of the cake. Cut into slices to serve.

TOP TIP
Instead of the buttercream topping, brush with a little warmed honey to give a sticky glaze.

Coconut & Lime Cake

SERVES 8

◆ Cooking time:
1–1¼ hours

INGREDIENTS

✳ 175 g/6 oz unsalted
butter, softened

✳ 175 g/6 oz caster sugar

✳ 3 eggs, beaten

✳ 150 g/5½ oz self-
raising flour

✳ 85 g/3 oz desiccated
coconut

✳ grated rind and juice of
1 lime

ICING

✳ 175 g/6 oz icing sugar

✳ grated rind and juice of
1 lime

✳ 25 g/1 oz shredded
coconut, lightly toasted

This quick and easy-to-bake cake has a lovely tropical-flavoured twist. It has a sweet and buttery coconut sponge which is complemented perfectly by a tangy lime icing.

1. Preheat the oven to 160ºC/325ºF/Gas Mark 3. Grease and line a 20-cm/8-inch round cake tin.

2. Place the butter and caster sugar in a large bowl and beat together until pale and fluffy. Gradually beat in the eggs. Sift in the flour and gently fold in using a metal spoon. Fold in the coconut, lime rind and juice.

3. Spoon the mixture into the prepared tin and smooth the surface. Bake in the preheated oven for 1–1¼ hours, or until risen, golden and firm to the touch. Cool in the tin for 5 minutes then turn out to cool completely on a wire rack.

4. For the icing, sift the icing sugar into a bowl. Stir in the lime rind and juice to make a thick smooth icing, adding a few drops of water, if necessary. Spoon the icing over the top of the cake, allowing it to drizzle down the sides of the cake. Scatter the toasted shredded coconut over the icing and leave to set.

TOP TIP
To extract the most juice from the limes,
roll the fruit firmly over a hard surface
before halving and squeezing.

Lemon Polenta Cake

SERVES 8

◆ Cooking time:
30–35 minutes

INGREDIENTS

✱ 200 g/7 oz unsalted
butter, plus extra
for greasing

✱ 200 g/7 oz caster sugar

✱ finely grated rind and
juice of 1 large lemon

✱ 3 eggs, beaten

✱ 140 g/5 oz ground
almonds

✱ 100 g/3½ oz quick-cook
polenta

✱ 1 tsp baking powder

✱ crème fraîche, to serve

SYRUP

✱ juice of 2 lemons

✱ 55 g/2 oz caster sugar

✱ 2 tbsp water

Polenta is a fine golden yellow cornmeal which is used in place of flour in this Italian cake. The result is a wonderfully soft dessert cake with a slightly crunchy texture.

1. Preheat the oven to 180°C/350°F/Gas Mark 4. Grease and line a 20-cm/8-inch round deep cake tin.

2. Beat the butter and sugar together until pale and fluffy. Beat in the lemon rind, lemon juice, eggs and ground almonds. Sift in the polenta and baking powder and stir until evenly mixed.

3. Spoon the mixture into the prepared tin and smooth the surface. Bake in the preheated oven for 30–35 minutes, or until just firm to the touch and golden brown. Remove the cake from the oven and leave to cool in the tin for 20 minutes.

4. To make the syrup, place the lemon juice, sugar and water in a small saucepan. Heat gently, stirring until the sugar has dissolved, then bring to the boil and simmer for 3–4 minutes, or until slightly reduced and syrupy. Turn out the cake onto a wire rack then brush half of the syrup evenly over the surface. Leave to cool completely.

5. Cut the cake into slices, drizzle the extra syrup over the top and serve with crème fraîche.

TOP TIP
This cake is best eaten warm on the day of making. It makes a lovely pudding when served with crème fraîche or double cream.

CHOCOLATE CAKES

3

Chocolate & Vanilla Ring

SERVES 12

◆ Cooking time:
40–50 minutes

INGREDIENTS

✳ oil or melted butter,
for greasing
✳ 175 g/6 oz plain
white flour
✳ 1 tbsp baking powder
✳ 175 g/6 oz unsalted
butter, softened
✳ 175 g/6 oz caster sugar
✳ 3 eggs, beaten
✳ 2 tbsp cocoa powder
✳ 2 tbsp milk
✳ 1 tsp vanilla extract
✳ icing sugar, for dusting

A marbled cake with swirls of contrasting sponges always looks impressive, but, when it is made in a ring-shaped tin, it looks even better!

1. Preheat the oven to 160°C/325°F/Gas Mark 3. Grease a 1.5-litre/2¾-pint ring cake tin.

2. Sift the flour and baking powder into a large bowl and add the butter, caster sugar and eggs. Beat well until the mixture is smooth. Transfer half the mixture to a separate bowl.

3. Mix the cocoa powder with the milk and stir into one bowl of mixture. Add the vanilla extract to the other bowl and mix evenly. Spoon alternate tablespoons of the two mixtures into the prepared tin and swirl lightly with a palette knife for a marbled effect.

4. Bake in the preheated oven for 40–50 minutes, or until risen, firm and golden brown. Leave to cool in the tin for 10 minutes, then turn out and finish cooling on a wire rack. Dust with icing sugar before serving.

TOP TIP
Take care not to over-swirl the mixture as you will lose the marbled effect.

Mocha Cake

SERVES 10–12

◆ Cooking time:
25–30 minutes

INGREDIENTS
* 225 g/8 oz self-raising flour
* 1 tsp baking powder
* 2 tbsp cocoa powder
* 225 g/8 oz butter, softened, plus extra for greasing
* 225 g/8 oz light soft brown sugar
* 4 large eggs, beaten
* 115 g/4 oz plain chocolate, melted
* 2 tbsp caster sugar
* 3 tbsp strong black coffee

FROSTING
* 85 g/3 oz unsalted butter, softened
* 250 g/9 oz mascarpone cheese
* 55 g/2 oz icing sugar
* 2 tbsp strong black coffee
* cocoa powder, to dust
* chocolate-coated coffee beans, to decorate

This delicious cake is the perfect combination of two classic flavours – chocolate and coffee.

1. Preheat the oven to 180°C/350°F/Gas Mark 4. Grease and line two 20-cm/8-inch sandwich tins.

2. Sift the flour, baking powder and cocoa powder into a large bowl. Add the butter, light soft brown sugar and eggs and, using an electric handheld whisk, beat together for 3–4 minutes, or until the mixture is very smooth and creamy. Fold in the melted chocolate.

3. Divide the mixture between the prepared cake tins and bake in the preheated oven for 25–30 minutes, or until risen and firm to the touch.

4. Place the caster sugar and black coffee in a small pan and heat gently for 1–2 minutes. Cool for 10 minutes. Pierce the tops of the warm cakes all over with a skewer and spoon the coffee syrup over the cakes. Leave the cakes to cool in the tins.

5. For the frosting, place the butter and mascarpone in a bowl and beat together until well blended. Beat in the icing sugar and coffee until smooth.

6. Remove the cakes from the tins and sandwich together with half the frosting. Swirl the remaining frosting over the top of the cake. Dust with cocoa powder and decorate with chocolate-coated coffee beans. Cut into slices to serve.

TOP TIP
Add a splash of coffee-flavoured liqueur to the warm syrup before spooning it over the cakes.

Red Velvet Cake

SERVES 12

✦ Cooking time:
25–30 minutes

INGREDIENTS

✹ 225 g/8 oz unsalted butter, plus extra for greasing
✹ 4 tbsp water
✹ 55 g/2 oz cocoa powder
✹ 3 eggs
✹ 250 ml/9 fl oz buttermilk
✹ 2 tsp vanilla extract
✹ 2 tbsp red edible food colouring
✹ 280 g/10 oz plain flour
✹ 55 g/2 oz cornflour
✹ 1½ tsp baking powder
✹ 280 g/10 oz caster sugar

FROSTING

✹ 250 g/9 oz cream cheese
✹ 40 g/1½ oz unsalted butter
✹ 3 tbsp caster sugar
✹ 1 tsp vanilla extract

A popular American cake with a rich buttermilk-flavoured chocolate sponge, it is coloured deep red by edible food colouring and topped off with a traditional vanilla cream cheese frosting.

1. Preheat the oven to 190°C/375°F/Gas Mark 5. Grease and line two 23-cm/9-inch sandwich tins.

2. Place the butter, water and cocoa powder in a small saucepan and heat gently, without boiling, stirring until melted and smooth. Remove from the heat and leave to cool slightly.

3. Beat together the eggs, buttermilk, vanilla extract and food colouring until frothy. Beat in the butter mixture. Sift together the flour, cornflour and baking powder, then stir quickly and evenly into the mixture with the caster sugar.

4. Spoon the mixture into the prepared tins and bake in the preheated oven for 25–30 minutes, or until risen and firm to the touch. Leave to cool in the tins for 3–4 minutes, then turn out onto a wire rack to cool completely.

5. To make the frosting, beat together all the ingredients until smooth. Use about half of the frosting to sandwich the cakes together, then spread the remainder over the top, swirling with a palette knife.

TOP TIP

Take care not to over-beat the cream cheese frosting as it can go a little runny. If this happens, chill in the refrigerator for 1 hour.

Chocolate & Sour Cherry Cake

SERVES 12

◆ Cooking time:
40–45 minutes

INGREDIENTS

✹ 175 g/6 oz plain
chocolate, broken
into pieces

✹ 115 g/4 oz butter,
diced, plus extra
for greasing

✹ 3 large eggs, separated

✹ 115 g/4 oz dark
muscovado sugar

✹ 115 g/4 oz self-raising
flour, sifted

✹ 55 g/2 oz ground
almonds

✹ 85 g/3 oz dried
cherries, chopped

✹ chocolate curls,
cocoa powder and fresh
cherries, to decorate

FROSTING

✹ 175 g/6 oz plain
chocolate, broken
into pieces

✹ 5 tbsp double cream

✹ 55 g/2 oz unsalted
butter

✹ 1 tbsp rum

An intensely dark and rich chocolate cake with a rum-flavoured chocolate frosting – this is definitely one for the grown ups. Serve with a dollop of crème fraîche for a delicious dessert.

1. Preheat the oven to 180°C/350°F/Gas Mark 4. Grease and line a 20-cm/8-inch round cake tin.

2. Place the chocolate and butter in a large heatproof bowl set over a saucepan of simmering water. Leave until melted. Remove from the heat and stir until smooth. Cool for 10 minutes, stirring occasionally.

3. Place the egg yolks and sugar in a large bowl and, using an electric handheld whisk, beat until pale and creamy. Add the melted chocolate and beat until thoroughly combined. Fold in the flour, ground almonds and dried cherries.

4. In a separate bowl, whisk the egg whites until soft peaks form then gently fold into the chocolate mixture. Spoon into the prepared tin and gently smooth the surface.

5. Bake in the preheated oven for 40–45 minutes, or until just firm to the touch and a skewer inserted into the centre comes out clean. Cool in the tin for 10 minutes then turn out onto a wire rack to cool completely.

6. For the frosting, place the chocolate, cream and butter in a heatproof bowl set over a saucepan of simmering water. Leave until melted, then remove from the heat and beat in the rum. Cool for 20 minutes then chill in refrigerator, stirring occasionally, for about 30 minutes or until thick enough to spread.

7. Spread the frosting over the top of the cake. Decorate with chocolate curls and dust lightly with cocoa powder. Top with cherries, slice and serve.

TOP TIP
For extra flavour, pierce the warm cake with a skewer and spoon over a little cherry liqueur.

Chocolate Ganache Cake

SERVES 10

◆ Cooking time: 40 minutes

INGREDIENTS

✳ 175 g/6 oz butter, plus extra for greasing
✳ 175 g/6 oz caster sugar
✳ 4 eggs, lightly beaten
✳ 250 g/9 oz self-raising flour
✳ 1 tbsp cocoa powder
✳ 50 g/1¾ oz plain chocolate, melted
✳ 200 g/7 oz chocolate-flavoured cake covering

GANACHE

✳ 450 ml/16 fl oz double cream
✳ 375 g/13 oz plain chocolate, broken into pieces

This impressive looking cake has a rich chocolate sponge and is decorated with a divinely glossy chocolate ganache. It takes a little time and skill to make but the effort will be well worth it.

1. Preheat the oven to 180°C/350°F/Gas Mark 4. Grease and line a 20-cm/8-inch round springform cake tin.

2. Beat the butter and sugar until light and fluffy. Gradually add the eggs, beating well after each addition. Sift the flour and cocoa powder together. Fold into the cake mixture. Fold in the melted chocolate.

3. Pour into the prepared tin and smooth the surface. Bake in the preheated oven for 40 minutes, or until springy to the touch. Leave the cake to cool for 5 minutes in the tin, then turn out onto a wire rack and leave to cool completely. Cut the cake into two layers.

4. To make the ganache, place the cream in a saucepan and bring to the boil, stirring. Add the chocolate and stir until melted. Pour into a bowl, leave to cool, then chill for 2 hours, or until set and firm. Whisk the mixture until light and fluffy.

5. Reserve one third of the ganache. Use the remaining ganache to sandwich the cake together and spread over the top and sides.

6. Melt the cake covering and spread it over a large sheet of baking paper. Leave to cool until just set. Cut into strips a little wider than the height. Place the strips around the edge of the cake, overlapping them slightly.

7. Pipe the reserved ganache in tear drops or shells to cover the top of the cake. Leave to chill for 1 hour.

TOP TIP

For a simpler decoration, spread the ganache smoothly over the top of the cake using a large palette knife and decorate with chocolate shavings.

SOMETHING SPECIAL

4

Boston Cream Pie

SERVES 10

◆ Cooking time:
20–25 minutes

INGREDIENTS
✳ 4 large eggs
✳ 115 g/4 oz caster sugar
✳ 115 g/4 oz plain flour
✳ 40 g/1½ oz butter,
melted and cooled,
plus extra for greasing

PASTRY CREAM
✳ 2 eggs
✳ 55 g/2 oz caster sugar
✳ 1 tsp vanilla extract
✳ 2 tbsp plain flour
✳ 2 tbsp cornflour
✳ 300 ml/10 fl oz milk
✳ 150 ml/5 fl oz double
cream, softly whipped

CHOCOLATE GLAZE
✳ 115 g/4 oz plain
chocolate, grated
✳ 1 tbsp golden syrup
✳ 25 g/1 oz unsalted
butter
✳ 150 ml/5 fl oz double
cream

Not a pie at all but an indulgent combination of two light sponge cakes, sandwiched with a rich vanilla pastry cream and topped with a glossy chocolate glaze.

1. Preheat the oven to 180°C/350°F/Gas Mark 4. Grease and line two 23-cm/9-inch sandwich tins.

2. Place the eggs and sugar in a heatproof bowl set over a saucepan of simmering water. Using an electric handheld whisk, beat together until the mixture is thick and pale and leaves a trail on the surface when the whisk is lifted.

3. Sift over the flour and fold in gently. Pour the butter in a thin stream over the mixture and fold in until just incorporated. Divide the mixture between the prepared tins and bake in the preheated oven for 20–25 minutes, or until light golden and springy to the touch. Cool in the tins for 5 minutes then turn out onto a wire rack to cool completely.

4. For the pastry cream, whisk together the eggs, sugar and vanilla extract. Blend the flour and cornflour to a paste with 4 tablespoons of the milk, then whisk into the egg mixture. Heat the remaining milk until almost boiling and pour onto the egg mixture, stirring all the

time. Return to the saucepan and cook over a low heat, whisking all the time, until smooth and thickened. Pour into a bowl, cover with dampened greaseproof paper. Leave until cold then fold in the whipped cream.

5. For the glaze, place the chocolate, golden syrup and butter in a heatproof bowl. Heat the cream until almost boiling then pour over the chocolate. Leave for 1 minute, then stir until smooth.

6. To assemble, sandwich the sponges together with the pastry cream. Spread the chocolate glaze over the top of the cake. Cut into slices to serve.

TOP TIP
Take care not to over-mix when folding in the flour and melted butter or the cake will have a heavy texture.

Sticky Ginger Loaf

SERVES 8–10

◆ Cooking time:
1–1¼ hours

INGREDIENTS

✳ oil or melted butter,
for greasing
✳ 175 g/6 oz plain
white flour
✳ 1 tbsp baking powder
✳ 1 tbsp ground ginger
✳ 175 ml/6 fl oz
sunflower oil
✳ 85 g/3 oz dark
muscovado sugar
✳ 85 g/3 oz golden syrup
✳ 3 eggs, beaten
✳ 3 pieces stem ginger in
syrup, drained and finely
chopped, plus 2 tbsp syrup
from the jar
✳ sliced stem ginger,
to decorate

This is a great cake for novice bakers to make as it is so easy – simply mix all the ingredients to a smooth batter, pour in the tin and bake! The sticky ginger topping transforms this standard loaf into something pretty and decorative.

1. Preheat the oven to 180°C/350°F/Gas Mark 4. Grease and line a 1.2-litre/2-pint loaf tin.

2. Sift the flour, baking powder and ground ginger into a large bowl. Add the oil, sugar, golden syrup and eggs, then beat well to a smooth batter. Stir in the chopped ginger.

3. Pour the mixture into the prepared tin. Bake in the preheated oven for 1–1¼ hours, or until well risen and firm.

4. Leave to cool in the tin for 10 minutes, then turn out and finish cooling on a wire rack. To serve, brush the top of the cake with the ginger syrup, decorate with sliced ginger and cut into slices.

TOP TIP

Leave golden syrup in a warm place
for 30 minutes before using to make it
easier to pour and measure.

Banoffee Pecan Cake

SERVES 6

◆ Cooking time:
25–30 minutes

INGREDIENTS
✳ oil or melted butter,
for greasing
✳ 175 g/6 oz plain
white flour
✳ 1 tbsp baking powder
✳ 175 g/6 oz unsalted
butter, softened
✳ 175 g/6 oz caster sugar
✳ 3 eggs, beaten
✳ 1 tsp vanilla extract
✳ 40 g/1½ oz pecan nuts,
finely chopped, plus extra
pecan halves to decorate
✳ 40 g/1½ oz dulce
de leche

FILLING & TOPPING
✳ 2 bananas
✳ 5 tbsp dulce de leche
✳ 100 ml/3½ fl oz double
cream

A variation on the classic dessert, this melt-in-the-mouth cake is an irresistible combination of rich caramel toffee, pecans, bananas and whipped cream!

1. Preheat the oven to 180°C/350°F/Gas Mark 4. Grease and line two 20-cm/8-inch sandwich tins.

2. Sift the flour and baking powder into a large bowl and add the butter, sugar, eggs and vanilla extract. Beat well until the mixture is smooth, then stir in the chopped pecans. Add the dulce de leche and stir to swirl through the mix.

3. Spoon the mixture into the prepared tins and smooth the surfaces with a palette knife. Bake in the preheated oven for 25–30 minutes, or until risen, firm and golden brown. Cool in the tins for 2–3 minutes, then turn out and finish cooling on a wire rack.

4. Reserve a few slices of banana for decoration and mash the remainder. Mix the mashed bananas with 3 tablespoons of the dulce de leche and use to sandwich the cakes together.

5. Whip the cream until thick, then swirl in the remaining dulce de leche. Spread over the cake and decorate with the reserved banana slices and the pecan halves.

TOP TIP
Brush the banana slices with a little lemon juice to stop them from browning before placing them on the top of the cake.

Squash & Orange Cake

SERVES 10–12

◆ Cooking time:
1 hour

INGREDIENTS

✳ 175 g/6 oz butter,
softened, plus extra
for greasing

✳ 175 g/6 oz light soft
brown sugar

✳ 3 eggs, beaten

✳ finely grated zest and
juice of 1 orange

✳ 225 g/8 oz self-raising
wholemeal flour

✳ 1 tsp baking powder

✳ 1 tsp ground cinnamon

✳ 225 g/8 oz prepared
butternut squash flesh
(peeled and deseeded
weight), roughly grated

✳ 115 g/4 oz sultanas

✳ pared orange zest,
to decorate

TOPPING

✳ 225 g/8 oz soft cheese

✳ 55 g/2 oz icing sugar,
sifted

Grated butternut squash gives this unusual cake a really moist and crumbly texture. Topped off with a tangy orange frosting it is a deliciously wholesome treat that everyone will love!

1. Preheat the oven to 180°C/350°F/Gas Mark 4. Grease and line an 18-cm/7-inch round deep cake tin.

2. Beat the butter and sugar together in a bowl until light and fluffy. Gradually beat in the eggs, beating well after each addition. Reserve 1 teaspoon of orange zest for the topping, then beat the remaining orange zest into the mixture.

3. Fold in the flour, baking powder and cinnamon, then fold in the squash, sultanas and a little orange juice, if necessary (about 1 tablespoon) to give a fairly soft consistency. Set aside the remaining orange juice. Spoon the mixture into the prepared tin and smooth the surface.

4. Bake in the preheated oven for about 1 hour, or until risen, firm to the touch and deep golden brown. Remove from the oven and cool in the tin for a few minutes, then turn out onto a wire rack. Remove the lining paper and leave to cool completely.

5. To make the topping, beat the soft cheese, icing sugar, reserved grated orange zest and 2–3 teaspoons of reserved orange juice together in a bowl until smooth and combined. Spread over the top of the cold cake, swirling it attractively, then sprinkle with pared orange zest. Serve immediately in slices.

TOP TIP

Because of its moist texture and soft cheese topping, this cake is best kept in the refrigerator and eaten within two days of making.

Grasshopper Cake

SERVES 8

◆ Cooking time:
1¼ hours

INGREDIENTS

✳ 250 ml/9 fl oz milk

✳ 1 tbsp lemon juice

✳ 280 g/10 oz self-raising flour

✳ 2 tbsp cocoa powder

✳ 1 tsp bicarbonate of soda

✳ 100 g/3½ oz butter, softened, plus extra for greasing

✳ 225 g/8 oz caster sugar

✳ 2 large eggs

✳ 100 g/3½ oz plain chocolate, melted

✳ 25 g/1 oz milk chocolate, grated, to decorate

FROSTING

✳ 200 g/7 oz unsalted butter, softened

✳ 250 ml/9 fl oz double cream

✳ 400 g/14 oz icing sugar, sifted

✳ 1 tsp peppermint extract

✳ few drops of green food colouring

Named after a Crème de Menthe cocktail, this decadent gateau is made up of layers of rich moist chocolate cake with a creamy mint-flavoured buttercream frosting.

1. Preheat the oven to 160°C/325°F/Gas Mark 3. Grease and line a 20-cm/8-inch round deep cake tin.

2. Pour the milk into a jug and add the lemon juice. Leave for 15 minutes – the milk will start to curdle but this is ok.

3. Sift the flour, cocoa powder and bicarbonate of soda into a large bowl. Add the butter, caster sugar and eggs and pour in the milk mixture. Beat with an electric handheld whisk until thoroughly combined. Whisk in the melted chocolate.

4. Spoon the mixture into the prepared tin and smooth the surface. Bake in the preheated oven for about 1¼ hours, or until the cake is risen and a skewer inserted into the centre comes out clean. Cool in the tin for 20 minutes then turn out onto a wire rack to cool completely.

5. For the frosting, place the butter in a bowl and beat with an electric handheld whisk for 2–3 minutes until pale and creamy. Beat in two thirds of the cream then gradually beat in the icing sugar. Add the rest of the cream and continue beating for 1–2 minutes until the buttercream is very light and fluffy. Stir in the peppermint extract and enough food colouring to give a pale green colour.

6. Slice the cake horizontally into three equal rounds. Sandwich the rounds together with half the buttercream frosting. Spread the remaining buttercream over the top and sides of the cake. Decorate with the chocolate shavings. Slice and serve.

TOP TIP

For an alcoholic version, flavour the buttercream with a couple of spoonfuls of Crème de Menthe instead of the peppermint extract.

White Chocolate & Coffee Cake

SERVES 8–10

◆ Cooking time:
25–30 minutes

INGREDIENTS

✳ 40 g/1½ oz unsalted butter, plus extra for greasing

✳ 85 g/3 oz white chocolate, broken into pieces

✳ 125 g/4½ oz caster sugar

✳ 4 large eggs, beaten

✳ 2 tbsp very strong black coffee

✳ 1 tsp vanilla extract

✳ 125 g/4½ oz plain flour

✳ white chocolate curls, to decorate

FROSTING

✳ 175 g/6 oz white chocolate, broken into pieces

✳ 85 g/3 oz unsalted butter

✳ 125 g/4½ oz crème fraîche

✳ 125 g/4½ oz icing sugar, sifted

✳ 1 tbsp coffee liqueur or very strong black coffee

Coffee and white chocolate go together particularly well in this decadent sponge gateau. Decorated with elegant chocolate curls, it is ideal to serve as an after-dinner dessert with coffee or liqueurs.

1. Preheat the oven to 180°C/350°F/Gas Mark 4. Grease and line two 20-cm/8-inch sandwich tins.

2. Place the butter and chocolate in a bowl set over a saucepan of hot, but not simmering, water and leave on a very low heat until just melted. Stir to mix lightly, then remove from the heat.

3. Place the caster sugar, eggs, coffee and vanilla extract in a large bowl set over a saucepan of hot water and whisk hard with an electric whisk until the mixture is pale and thick enough to leave a trail when the whisk is lifted.

4. Remove from the heat, sift in the flour and fold in lightly and evenly. Quickly fold in the butter and chocolate mixture, then divide the mixture between the prepared tins.

5. Bake in the preheated oven for 25–30 minutes, or until risen, golden brown and springy to the touch. Leave to cool in the tins for 2 minutes, then run a knife around the edges to loosen and turn out onto a wire rack to cool.

6. For the frosting, place the chocolate and butter in a bowl set over a saucepan of hot water and heat gently until melted. Remove from the heat, stir in the crème fraîche, then add the icing sugar and coffee liqueur and mix until smooth. Chill the frosting for at least 30 minutes, stirring occasionally, until it becomes thick and glossy.

7. Use about one third of the frosting to sandwich the cakes together. Spread the remainder over the top and sides, swirling with a palette knife. Arrange the chocolate curls over the top of the cake and leave to set.

TOP TIP

For chocolate curls, spread melted white chocolate onto a clean flat surface. Leave to set, then drag a thin blade across the surface at a slight angle.

Blueberry Swirl Cake

SERVES 8–10

◆ Cooking time:
20–25 minutes

INGREDIENTS

✹ oil or melted butter,
for greasing

✹ 175 g/6 oz plain
white flour

✹ 1 tbsp baking powder

✹ 175 g/6 oz unsalted
butter, softened

✹ 175 g/6 oz caster sugar

✹ 3 eggs, beaten

✹ 1 tsp orange
flower water

✹ 2 tbsp orange juice

FILLING & FROSTING

✹ 200 g/7 oz soft cheese

✹ 100 g/3½ oz icing
sugar, sifted

✹ 225 g/8 oz fresh
blueberries

This cake has a lovely fragrant orange flavour and a creamy frosting swirled with fresh blueberry purée. It is delicious served as a simple summer dessert or teatime treat.

1. Preheat the oven to 160°C/325°F/Gas Mark 3. Grease and line three 20-cm/8-inch sandwich tins.

2. Sift the flour and baking powder into a large bowl and add the butter, caster sugar, eggs and orange flower water. Beat well until the mixture is smooth, then stir in the orange juice.

3. Spoon the mixture into the prepared tins and smooth the surfaces with a palette knife. Bake in the preheated oven for 20–25 minutes, or until risen, firm and golden brown.

4. Leave to cool in the tins for 2–3 minutes, then turn out and finish cooling on a wire rack.

5. For the frosting, beat together the soft cheese and icing sugar until smooth. Transfer about two thirds of the mixture to a separate bowl and stir in 140 g/5 oz of the blueberries, then use this to sandwich the cakes together.

6. Rub the remaining blueberries through a fine sieve to make a smooth purée. Spread the remaining frosting on top of the cake and swirl the blueberry purée through it.

TOP TIP
Add a splash of orange flower
water to the frosting for an extra
boost of flavour.

Frosted Raspberry Almond Ring

SERVES 8–10

◆ Cooking time:
40–45 minutes

INGREDIENTS

✳ oil or melted butter, for greasing
✳ 175 g/6 oz plain white flour
✳ 1 tbsp baking powder
✳ 175 g/6 oz unsalted butter, softened
✳ 175 g/6 oz caster sugar
✳ 3 eggs, beaten
✳ 1 tsp almond extract
✳ 70 g/2½ oz ground almonds
✳ 225 g/8 oz fresh raspberries
✳ toasted flaked almonds, to decorate

FROSTING

✳ 1 large egg white
✳ 140 g/5 oz icing sugar
✳ 1 tbsp golden syrup
✳ ¼ tsp cream of tartar

Cakes made in a ring cake tin always look impressive and this delicious almond and raspberry cake is no exception. The fresh fruit and frosting topping finish this cake off beautifully and make it a perfect dessert for a dinner party.

1. Preheat the oven to 160°C/325°F/Gas Mark 3. Grease a 1.5-litre/2¾-pint ring cake tin.

2. Sift the flour and baking powder into a large bowl and add the butter, caster sugar, eggs and almond extract. Beat well until the mixture is smooth, then stir in the ground almonds. Mash half the raspberries with a fork and stir into the mixture.

3. Spoon the mixture into the prepared tin and smooth the surface with a palette knife. Bake in the preheated oven for 40–45 minutes, or until risen, firm and golden brown.

4. Leave to cool in the tin for 10 minutes, then turn out carefully onto a wire rack to finish cooling.

5. For the frosting, place the egg white, icing sugar, golden syrup and cream of tartar in a bowl over a saucepan of hot water and beat vigorously with an electric handheld mixer until thick enough to hold its shape.

6. Swirl the frosting over the top of the cake. Decorate with the remaining raspberries and the flaked almonds.

TOP TIP

If you are using a cake tin that doesn't have a non-stick coating, place a thin strip of baking paper in the base of the greased tin.

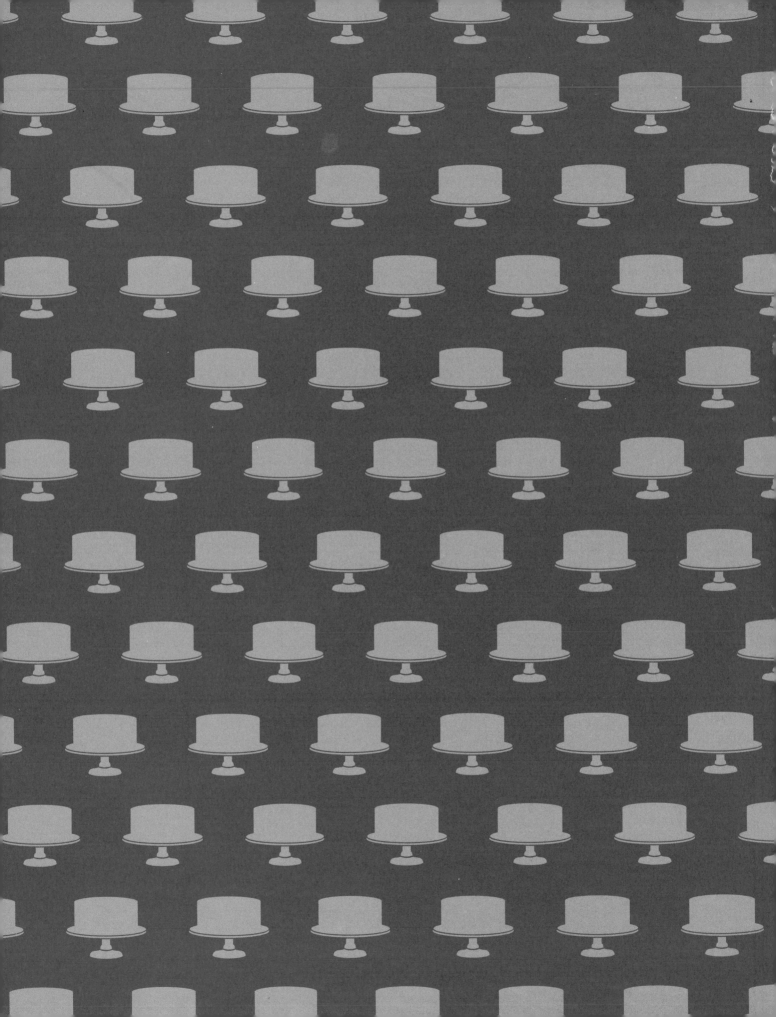